Fabric Collage Quilts

Fabric Collage Quilts

Using Creative Appliqué and Embellishments

JOANNE GOLDSTEIN

Martingale
& COMPANY

BOTHELL, WASHINGTON

CREDITS

President . . . . Nancy J. Martin

CEO/Publisher . . . . Daniel J. Martin

Associate Publisher . . . . Jane Hamada

Editorial Director . . . . Mary V. Green

Design and Production Manager . . . .Cheryl Stevenson

Technical Editor . . . . Karen C. Soltys

Copy Editor .Tina Cook

Illustrator . . . . Laurel Strand

Photographer . . . . .Brent Kane

Cover and Text Designer . . . . .Trina Stahl

Fabric Collage Quilts: Using Creative Appliqué and
Embellishments
© 1999 by Joanne Goldstein
Martingale & Company
PO Box 118
Bothell, WA 98041-0118 USA
www.patchwork.com

Printed in Hong Kong
04 03 02 01 00 99   6 5 4 3 2

That Patchwork Place is an imprint of
Martingale & Company.

MISSION STATEMENT

*We are dedicated to providing quality products
and service by working together to inspire creativity
and to enrich the lives we touch.*

Library of Congress Cataloging-in-Publication Data
Goldstein, Joanne,
Fabric collage quilts : using creative appliqué and
embellishments / Joanne Goldstein.
p.   cm.
ISBN 1-56477-263-2
1. Patchwork.   2. Quilting.   3. Appliqué.
I. Title.
TT835.G655   1999
746.46'041—dc21   99-25296
                                             CIP

FACING PAGE: FABULOUS FLORIDA *by Joanne Goldstein, 1998, Coral Springs, Florida, 53½ " x 66½ ".*
Lots of traditional appliqué creates a Floridian background. Dark borders give the colorful fabric motifs a visual boost.

DEDICATION

❧

To Grandma, who is forever in my heart.

ACKNOWLEDGMENTS

❧

I GRATEFULLY EXTEND my gratitude to the staff of Martingale & Company for taking a chance on a first-time author.

Thank you to the members of Coral Springs Quilters for your enthusiastic response to my quilts, and especially to the Thursday Evening Quilt Bee for your encouragement, interest, and support.

Special, heartfelt thanks go to my family: Steven, for patiently answering my million and one questions, giving technical advice, sharing your photographic expertise, and making me look good! Lauren, for your input, constant encouragement, and unfailing ability to advise and critique with a gentle nudge in the right direction. And especially, thank you for all the times you told me that you are proud of me. Thank you, David, my computer genius, for your patience, for sharing your amazing computer abilities, and for your interest in my work. Most of all, thank you for taking me by the hand and pulling me into the twenty-first century. And to my husband, Jerry, thank you for giving me the courage to try—without you, there would be no me!

Contents

❦

Introction

I LOVE FABRIC! Walking into any fabric shop alerts my senses. Inspiration infuses my brain and my creative juices begin to flow. Not only do I love fabric, I also enjoy every aspect of needlework. All kinds of floss, ribbon, beads, lace, and thread excite me. My fabric closet is bulging, but I am constantly on the lookout for unusual fabrics and unique prints to add to my collection. This compulsion to purchase fabric causes my husband to shudder, but it gets my pulse racing.

The look and feel of traditional patchwork has always fascinated me. However, after years of sewing traditional pieced and appliquéd quilts, I had an overwhelming desire to create something fresh and new. My adventure into art quilts began with some chintz yardage of huge chrysanthemums. I didn't want to cut up those gorgeous blooms, but the fabric was too beautiful not to use, so I cut out the individual motifs and used them as appliqués.

Soon, I began to notice the wide variety of large-scale prints that were available in fabric stores. I started with beautiful floral motifs, then added colorful bird, fish, butterfly, and other nature fabrics to create quilts that rivaled paintings. Traditionally pieced backgrounds became my canvas, and fabric motifs and colorful threads became the paint!

Of course, using printed fabrics for appliqué isn't a new idea. Broderie perse, in which motifs are cut from a cotton fabric and embroidered onto a solid background, dates back to the nineteenth century. At that time, it was common to use flowers, leaves, and birds found on popular chintz fabrics. These motifs were applied to the background with a decorative blanket stitch, or the edges were turned under and secured with a tiny blind stitch. These early appliqué quilts are almost exclusively floral designs.

What's exciting to me is combining the nineteenth-century broderie perse technique with today's wonderful quilt and specialty fabrics, then adding a touch—or two!—of embellishment. When viewed from afar, these quilts are beautiful, colorful works of art. But when examined up close, a wealth of embroidery, beads, silk ribbons, and lace embellishments invite detailed inspection.

This is not meant to be a book of patterns, but rather a book of ideas that will take you through the adventure of creating your own art quilts. Look for inspiration all around you. Books, photographs, postcards, and greeting cards can spark wonderful ideas. Just remember to trust your creativity, and don't be afraid to experiment. You can create spectacular still lifes, landscapes, and seascapes by using the

TROPICAL GARDEN *by Joanne Goldstein, 1998, Coral Springs, Florida, 50½" x 51½".*
Pieced half-square triangles give the water background shimmering depth. Colorful theme fabrics fill the garden with birds, frogs, lizards, insects, and flowers.

techniques in *Fabric Collage Quilts.* But don't let your imagination stop there. Explore fantasy, animal, holiday, and children's quilts, and any other themes you can dream up. Nothing is impossible, and thinking of new ways to use fabric can be an adventure in itself.

The best way to use this book is to read the general instructions to familiarize yourself with fabric-collage techniques. Practice the Confidence Builder exercises sprinkled throughout the book, look at the photos for inspiration, then create your own quilts using the project guidelines on pages 67–87. You'll find step-by-step directions for three quilts: "Floral Elegance," a beautiful floral bouquet; "Tea Time," a charming still life; and "Shangri-La," a striking landscape design. These quilts may look difficult, but the techniques are easy to master.

No art training, drawing ability, or designer know-how is needed for you to create spectacular quilts. Lush still lifes, rich woodlands, exotic rain forests, and incredible animals are all there in the fabric shop waiting for you to snip, fuse, and create. Your progress will be rapid and the results beautiful. And, as you begin to collect fabrics, I guarantee that the ideas will begin to flow. Search out theme fabrics and let them inspire you. Trust your intuitive design ability and you won't go wrong.

While quilters of any skill level can use the techniques in this book, I've assumed that you have a general knowledge of quilting. If you feel you need help with basic piecing and quilting, refer to the Bibliography on page 94 for books on beginning quiltmaking.

I machine-piece the backgrounds for my quilts, but I appliqué (with some help from fusible web), embroider, and quilt by hand. However, if you're a machine enthusiast, you can certainly use machine techniques for most of the work on these quilts.

So, get out your beautiful fabrics and scraps, and pull that fantastic floral or underwater fabric you've been saving off the shelf. Now is the time to use those gorgeous new threads. Sift through your collection of beads, buttons, and lace. It's time to start thinking about the wonderful work of art you're going to create.

Shopping List

❧

As with any project, you need to gather your materials and supplies before you begin. If you're already a quilter, you probably have most of the supplies on hand. You may not need every item mentioned here for the quilt you want to make, but read through the list so you'll be sure to have what you do need and not have to run out to the quilt shop as you work.

Background fabric: Use 100% cotton fabrics for your quilt's pieced background. Try to have a variety of fabrics on hand to audition. Check out your favorite fabric shop's medley of fat quarters to economically build your collection. Refer to "Background Fabric" on pages 25–29 for more information.

Theme fabric: A theme fabric can be any printed fabric that includes design motifs you can use as appliqués. Refer to "Theme Fabric" on pages 23–25 for everything you need to know, including how much to buy.

Thread for piecing: For machine piecing, use cotton or cotton-covered polyester sewing thread. Try using a medium gray thread in both the needle and bobbin. Since gray blends beautifully with most fabric, you won't have to change thread frequently.

Embroidery floss: For freezer-paper appliqué, one strand of embroidery floss in a quilting needle makes a neat and invisible appliqué stitch. The floss is soft, easy to sew with, and sinks into the background fabric with just a slight tug. In addition, floss is available in such a wide variety of colors that it is easy to closely match any fabric.

Thread for blanket stitching: Embroidery floss is also perfect for blanket stitches, but don't limit yourself! Experiment with variegated floss, metallic floss, rayon and silk threads, perle cotton, narrow silk ribbon, and machine-embroidery thread. Buy floss and threads at the same time you buy your fabric so you can easily match, coordinate, and contrast colors. Combine different threads in the same quilt for variety, texture, and interest.

Fusible web: You'll use paper-backed fusible web to apply theme-fabric motifs to your quilt. There are many brands on the market. Choose a lightweight web that will be easy to embroider through. To ensure a secure bond, it is important that you follow the manufacturer's instructions. If, in the course of handling the quilt top, some of the fused pieces come loose, simply re-fuse them with a hot iron.

Pins: Use ¾" sequin pins to keep your appliqués in place. Although these tiny pins take some getting used to, I find they are the best for appliqué. They remain securely pinned in the fabric and don't get in the way as you stitch.

Needles: Quilting Betweens are great for both hand appliqué and hand quilting. Try using a size 8 Between for quilting through the motifs—smaller needles can break easily when you quilt through multiple layers. For embroidering with floss, use a size 7 or 8 Embroidery needle. For embroidering with decorative thread or silk ribbon, try Chenille needles in various sizes to accommodate different threads.

Embroidery hoop: Use a wooden or plastic 8" hoop with a tightening hinge. An 8" hoop is large enough to encompass most motifs and small enough to manipulate comfortably.

Silk ribbon: Use silk ribbon to add leaves, small flowers, grass, and stems to your quilts. To embroider accents of different sizes, try 4mm, 7mm, and 13mm ribbons.

Beads: Use seed beads to add sparkle to flowers, underwater scenes, and landscapes. Bugle beads make great twigs, stems, and small leaves. If you haven't used beads on a quilt before, you'll be delighted at the texture and highlights they can add. I try to use beads in all my quilts.

Beading needle and thread: Use a long, slender Beading needle and strong beading thread, such as Nymo, to secure all beadwork.

Freezer paper: Use this grocery-store item to make templates for hand appliqué.

Bias bars: Metal or plastic bars that come in sets of varying widths will help you create consistently sized bias strips for appliquéd vines, branches, and stems.

Permanent pens: Brown and black Pigma pens, size .05, are best for drawing fine details on fabric.

Water-soluble pen: Use a water-soluble pen to mark embroidery designs on your quilt top. The markings will remain on the quilt top until washed out.

Basic quilting supplies: You'll need your sewing machine, rotary cutter, a rotary-cutting mat and ruler, sewing pins, and small appliqué scissors.

Design materials: To design your quilt, you need drawing paper, a water-soluble glue-stick, and markers.

Embellishments: Collect buttons, lace doilies, old tablecloths and linens, netting, and other treasures to include in your quilt. It's easy to overwhelm a quilt with embellishments, so remember, a little goes a long way!

Batting: Choose a thin, low-loft batting, or try lightweight fleece.

Confidence Builder 1

ALL THIS TALK about supplies may have you anxious to get started. But before we move on, let's try our first Confidence Builder. Use the following exercise to develop your design ability.

Purchase one small piece (about ½ yard), or several smaller pieces of different theme prints. Choose colorful and unusual fabrics that you might not ordinarily use in your quilts. Cut out several motifs and place them on a large piece of drawing paper. Play with the arrangement until a pleasing design emerges. Using a marker, outline a shape on which to anchor your pieces, such as a vase, tabletop, or body of water. If you like, you can draw additional design elements.

When you're happy with your design, lightly dab a water-soluble gluestick on the back of the fabric motifs and glue them to the paper. Then set your design aside and start a new one on another piece of paper. Continue experimenting with the arrangement of the fabric motifs and adding other design elements with your markers until you feel comfortable with the process. Since you are using printed fabric motifs with realistic imagery, the design elements that you add with your markers can be simple. Save all your designs to use later with other Confidence Builder exercises.

Color

Beautiful construction and superb technique do not guarantee success. A quilter may bring to her work years of experience and sewing proficiency, but if she also makes poor color choices she'll probably produce a less-than-exciting quilt. On the other hand, an inexperienced quilter who chooses color effectively can produce a spectacular work of art.

Choosing a color scheme strikes fear in the hearts of many quilters, but learning the basics of color theory will make it easy for you to build theme fabrics into a coordinated fabric palette.

THE COLOR WHEEL

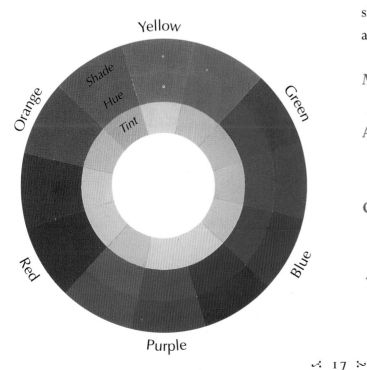

Believe it or not, most of us have a natural color instinct. Learning a few simple color principles can turn that instinct into color confidence.

You're probably already familiar with the basics of color theory. There are three primary colors—red, yellow, and blue. Mixing equal amounts of any two primary colors produces secondary colors—orange, green, and purple. Mixing a primary and a secondary color produces a tertiary color—yellow-orange, blue-green, red-purple, and so on, as shown in the color wheel at left. You won't find black, white, or brown on the color wheel. They work as neutrals in color schemes, helping to ease the transition between other colors. So use any of them as needed in your quilt.

There are four basic color schemes:

Monochromatic—various tints and shades of a single color.

Analogous—neighboring colors on the color wheel, such as blue, blue-green, and green, or red, red-purple, and purple.

Complementary—colors that lie opposite one another on the color wheel, such as blue and orange, or red and green.

Triadic—three colors that form a triangle on the color wheel, such as red, yellow, and blue; or orange, green, and purple.

Colors can be separated into two temperatures: cool and warm. Blue, green, and purple (think sky and water) are cool colors. Red, yellow, and orange (think earth and fire) are warm. The temperature of a color affects the mood and energy of a design. Cool colors are calm and peaceful; warm colors are wild and exciting.

In addition to classic color schemes, it helps to know a few color terms. *Intensity* is the brightness or dullness of a color. Each color is brightest in its pure state, with no black, white, or other colors blended into it. A color

becomes duller when it is mixed with its complementary color. For example, to dull down red, you would add green. A color reaches its dullest intensity when an equal amount of its complementary color is added to it.

Value is the relative lightness or darkness of a color. Light colors advance and dark colors recede, a fact that becomes especially important when you're choosing background fabrics.

When white is added to a color it becomes a *tint;* adding black darkens it to a *shade.* Just to complicate things, colors react to other colors

CORAL REEF *by Joanne Goldstein, 1997, Coral Springs, Florida, 34" x 30". Warm-hued fish and coral make their home in a background of cool blues. The contrast of color and temperature heightens the drama of the scene.*

around them. A color can appear darker or lighter, brighter or duller in response to its neighbors. To create strong color combinations, include different intensities, values, tints, and shades in your quilts.

YOUR COLOR PALETTE

When planning the color palette for your quilt, think of your project as two separate quilts (the pieced background and the picture foreground) that are color-dependent on one another. Neither area can stand on its own, but when combined they produce a striking work of art.

Let your theme fabric be your color guide. Since the focus of your quilt will be the theme-fabric collage, choose the theme fabric first. You may even want to use several theme fabrics. You will cut the motifs from their backgrounds, so it's important to not be overly influenced or limited by the background color. For example, let's say you've chosen a sunflower print as your theme fabric. The sunflowers vary from light yellow to gold, ochre, and orange, and the background is dark green. Looking at that print, it will be hard to imagine the sunflowers against anything but green.

To help you to visually separate a motif from its background, cut a window from the middle of an index card or piece of sturdy paper. Make window templates of several sizes. Take these handy tools with you when you shop for fabric and use them to isolate and preview motifs without the distraction of background colors or adjacent motifs.

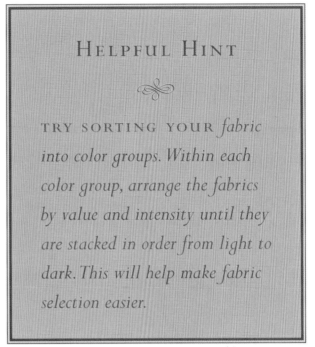

HELPFUL HINT

TRY SORTING YOUR fabric into color groups. Within each color group, arrange the fabrics by value and intensity until they are stacked in order from light to dark. This will help make fabric selection easier.

Use window templates to isolate motifs.

With practice, you will be able to visualize the motif separately from the background. Work your way through Confidence Builder 2 on the following page to see the effects different background colors can have on motifs.

THE POTTING SHED *by Joanne Goldstein, 1998, Coral Springs, Florida, 52½" x 58".*
Complementary reds and greens predominate, and orange-gold and yellow, which are analogous to red on the color wheel,
round out the color scheme. A variety of values and intensities keep the palette engaging: medium-value leaves stand out against
the darks and lights of the background, and bright red and pink geraniums sing amid duller brick reds.

Confidence Builder 2

SORT THROUGH YOUR fabric stash for a floral or novelty print, then cut a few motifs from it. Position the motifs on a variety of background fabrics, auditioning different colors and combinations of colors to see how the motifs interact with the assorted backgrounds.

You can also use the designs you created in Confidence Builder 1 (page 15). Using colored pencils or crayons, fill in the various design elements that you drew. Notice how your fabric pictures come alive when you add color. Try different background colors for each of your designs.

As you experiment with different colors, you'll notice that some blues appear greener and certain reds seem more orange when placed next to other colors. Some colors may appear brighter and more vibrant in relation to others, and subtle variations of shade you hadn't previously noticed might appear.

After playing with different color schemes, you'll notice that certain combinations work better than others. When choosing colors for your quilts, keep in mind that quilts with contrast are the most interesting. If the motifs don't contrast well with the background, the design will get lost.

Audition a variety of fabrics to see how your motifs react to different backgrounds.

Choosing Fabrics

❧

SELECTING QUILT FABRICS is fun—maybe even the best part of the quiltmaking process! Think of your project as two separate but closely related quilts. One is the pieced background; the other is the foreground picture. Together, they form a beautiful quilt.

THEME FABRICS

The most important fabric in a collage quilt is the theme fabric, or fabrics. Some fabric shops call them novelty prints, conversation prints, or fashion fabrics. Whatever the name, any fabric with well-defined motifs can be used as a theme fabric. Potential theme fabrics are easy to spot—just look for colorful, eye-catching images: jumping frogs, cascading flowers, swimming dolphins, floating water lilies. I love to search for and collect these fabrics, and admittedly, the task is getting easier. More and more exciting prints, in increasing variety, are coming on the market all the time.

The more theme fabrics you have on hand, the more flexible you can be while you design your quilt. Try to collect motifs of different sizes. Variety of scale makes it easier to add perspective, depth, and diversity to your design, all of which add up to eye appeal.

As you build your theme-fabric library, look for interesting accent motifs. You may be working

Theme fabrics offer exciting design possibilities.

Collect large, medium, and small motifs.

life in another, fruits in a third. That way, when you're designing a landscape, it will be easy to find that perfect butterfly or bird you need.

When it comes to theme fabrics, you don't have to limit yourself to quilting cottons. Rayon, silk, challis, and other dress fabrics are excellent sources of unusual and colorful prints. Since you'll be cutting out the motifs and fusing them to a background rather than piecing them, you can use almost any fabric successfully.

For instance, dressmaker fabrics can add a beautiful shimmer and sparkle you can't achieve with cotton alone. Lustrous fabrics are especially nice to use in tropical scenes, seascapes, and landscapes. Combining different types of fabrics gives you an opportunity to create wonderful textural contrasts.

You don't have to stop with fashion fabrics. Some decorator fabrics are also suitable for art quilts. If you decide to include a decorator fabric in your quilt, wash it at least three times in hot water with regular laundry detergent before fusing it to your quilt background. Dry the fabric in a hot dryer between each wash. If it doesn't soften after three hot-water washes, use the fabric only if you're going to machine quilt your top. It would be difficult to hand quilt through multiple layers of heavy fabric.

Yardage for Theme Fabrics

Purchase your theme fabrics first. The amount of theme fabric to buy depends on the size of the motifs and how often they repeat. As a guide, if the motif is 1" to 2" in size and repeats closely, one yard will be enough. Remember, you'll be cutting out the design motifs with a ¼" seam allowance. So, if the design motifs touch or are so close together that there isn't space for

on a still-life quilt, but the addition of birds and insects will help make it an interesting composition. A varied theme-fabric collection is the best way to ensure a successful quilt.

Organize your theme fabrics by subject. For example, stack florals together in one pile, sea a ¼" seam allowance around each one, you'll need to increase the yardage. If the motifs are large—3" or more—and the repeats are spaced 3" to 6" or more apart, you'll need approximately two yards of fabric. Of course, the amount you need also depends on how many of the motifs you plan to incorporate into your quilt. If you need just one large cabbage rose, ¼ or ⅓ yard may be enough. If you want a whole cottage garden of cabbage roses, then you'll probably need one or two yards.

BACKGROUND FABRICS

Piecing the background of your quilt rather than using a single fabric creates visual interest. For fabric lovers, fabric hoarders, and compulsive fabric shoppers, this is an excellent opportunity to use a variety of different fabrics. A wealth of opportunity can be found in your fabric stash.

Use 100% cotton fabric for all background piecing. Start with a mental picture of your appliqué design and choose background fabrics that complement that foreground picture. In general, aim for contrast between the two parts of your quilt. Dark backgrounds highlight the fabric picture and are visually dynamic; light backgrounds are calm and subtle. Either approach can produce dramatic effects in your quilt.

Plaids, small prints, narrow stripes, and pin dots are excellent choices for background blocks. Try to incorporate solids and near-solids (subtle tone-on-tone prints) in your blocks to allow a place for your eye to rest.

Solids and near-solids work well in a pieced background.

These fabrics are too busy for a pieced background.

STILL LIFE WITH FRUIT *by Joanne Goldstein, 1998, Coral Springs, Florida, 54" x 45".*
Pieced blocks add subtle movement to this dark background.

Cut several motifs from your theme-fabric stash and take them with you when you go fabric shopping. Place them against different fabrics to audition them for the background. Keep in mind that small-scale prints in the background complement large-scale motifs in the foreground. Varying the scale between the background and the theme motifs ensures a balanced mix of fabrics. Remember, the background is

meant to be a canvas on which you can "paint" your design with fabric motifs, not a show-stopping, stand-alone patchwork quilt.

I love the look of traditional quilt blocks and try to include them in my backgrounds; however, you can also get excellent results with trapunto, crazy quilting, and appliqué, or with a combination of these techniques. A whole-cloth background made from one interesting print

CHRYSANTHEMUMS *by Joanne Goldstein, 1998, Coral Springs, Florida, 45" x 54".*
Soft, neutral background blocks make an excellent foil for colorful motifs.

can also be dramatic—try hand-dyed and marbled fabrics. You can find many fabrics that simulate the look of sky, water, grass, or trees, and these make especially impressive landscape backgrounds. Experiment with different fabrics and techniques, but remember that the more interesting the background, the more appealing your quilt will be. Just don't make your background so dynamic that it will compete with your collage motifs.

SUNFLOWERS *by Joanne Goldstein, 1997, Coral Springs, Florida, 57" x 50". I usually design a subtle background, but with this quilt I opted for high-contrast piecing. The vibrant Evening Star blocks might easily have overwhelmed the quieter window area, but quilted clouds add movement, balancing the design.*

Yardage for the Background

Fat quarters are easy to find and collect, and they make great additions to your fabric stash. You'll be amazed at how fast your fabric collection grows when you buy a few fat quarters each time you visit a quilt shop. Using fat quarters will give your background patchwork a scrappy look, because you'll need a variety of them to create a large background.

If you buy your background fabric off the bolt, purchase at least one yard to make sure you have enough fabric to complete all the piecing. There's nothing worse than running out, and you can always find a way to use any leftover fabric!

I don't like to limit my creativity by establishing a set amount of fabric to purchase. I try to use many different fabrics in my backgrounds. It makes my quilts interesting and dimensional, and scraps never go to waste. Always allow extra yardage for your borders,

backing, and binding, too. You never know—what you planned as a simple vase of flowers may bloom into a much larger bouquet. If you're unsure about the final size of your design, it may be best to purchase border, backing, and binding fabrics after you've completed the appliqué portion of your quilt.

> ## HELPFUL HINT
>
> DON'T FORGET TO *buy any additional fabric you might need for large appliqués like vases, tables, trees, rocks, and bushes.*

Creating a Fabric Collage Quilt

DESIGNING A QUILT is like embarking on an adventure. You may not have a definite itinerary, and you never know what obstacles will present themselves along the way. You may not even know where your journey will lead, but one thing is sure. It's going to be a fun and exciting learning experience.

THE FABRIC CANVAS

Piece the background of your quilt either by hand or machine. If possible, use Template-Free® rotary-cutting techniques to speed up the process and ensure accuracy.

Quilts that measure 50" to 60" per side give you a generous fabric canvas on which you can design. Smaller sizes can also be effective as long as your motifs are in proportion to the overall size of the quilt.

Choose simple, traditional blocks for your background, such as any of the classic designs illustrated at right.

If you'd prefer to create your own block design, just remember to keep it simple. You don't want your pieced background to compete with the appliqués you'll add later.

A block that measures from 6" to 10" square is generally a good size to use for the pieced background. On a 60" quilt, this size allows for enough repeats to establish a pattern without overwhelming the theme-fabric motifs. If, after you've completed several blocks, the design seems too busy, set the blocks with plain solid or

Nine Patch

Square-in-a-Square

Bow Tie

Evening Star

Rail Fence

Churn Dash

Jacob's Ladder

Pine Tree

Ohio Star

Shoo Fly

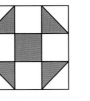
Friendship Star

Log Cabin

SIMPLE PLEASURES *by Joanne Goldstein, 1998, Coral Springs, Florida, 37" x 32". This small quilt uses medium- and small-scale motifs that might have disappeared against a larger background.*

tone-on-tone print squares to quiet the design. If you use alternate squares, keep the color contrast low. Remember, this is only the background of the quilt. Aim for a subtle, interesting arrangement of blocks with areas of calm.

Another contemporary piecing approach is to construct one large block that measures the entire size of the quilt. This is particularly striking on quilts that measure approximately 40" square. Try a simple block, such as Square-in-a-Square, using the center square of the block for your collage. See "Floral Elegance" on page 69 for an example of this technique.

ADDING BORDERS

Complete all the appliqué and embroidery before you attach the borders. Borders would just be more fabric you'd have to manipulate, and it's not unusual for a quilt top to become distorted from the embroidery and all the handling it gets as you repeatedly put it in a hoop. When you're finished with the embroidery, square up the quilt top (see page 57), and then add borders. My only exception to this rule is if the appliqué design extends into the borders, as in "A Country Garden" on page 35.

DESIGNING THE FABRIC PICTURE

Once your background is complete, you're ready to create the pictorial design. Don't worry if you've never designed your own quilt before.

It's not hard to create a quilt that looks elaborate and sophisticated—theme fabric makes it easy. If you're not confident of your design abilities, it may help to work from a sketch or photo.

Creating Appliqué Shapes

You can appliqué shapes to fabric in a variety of ways. I use freezer-paper templates and appliqué by hand, and instructions for those techniques follow.

Hang your background on a design wall or spread it out on the floor. Lay large pieces of freezer paper over the quilt and draw outlines of any design elements you want to include, such as vases, baskets, or rolling hills. Keep the shapes simple, and be careful not to poke your pen or pencil through the paper (you don't want to mark your quilt background).

Don't worry about drawing perfect shapes. The simpler your design, the more effective your composition will be, since the fabric motifs will be the focus of the finished quilt. Cut out the freezer-paper templates, position them on your quilt, and pin them in place.

Pin freezer-paper shapes to the background.

Confidence Builder 3

❧

MAKE SOME BACKGROUND blocks, then arrange them as desired on a design wall or on the floor. Cut some motifs from the theme fabric. Don't worry about attaching fusible web to them. At this point, you're just practicing and may not even use these shapes in the quilt top. Pin the motifs to the background in random positions. Aim for contrast and balance between the motifs and the background. Let the quilt blocks remain in place for a few days. Continue to rearrange the blocks until you're completely satisfied with the background.

Sew the blocks together in rows, then join the rows. Carefully and thoroughly clip all loose threads, then press your background. To make certain the background is "square," measure it from side to side and from top to bottom through the center. Since the edges may have stretched, measuring through the center is more accurate than measuring the edges themselves. *After* measuring through the center, measure the edges. If the measurements differ by more than

½", adjust seams to fix the problem. If the difference is less than ½", you should be able to fix the discrepancy by easing in the extra when you attach borders.

Squaring up is an important step that you shouldn't skip. You want to be sure that the background is perfectly square before you begin the surface design; otherwise, all your hard work will result in a lopsided quilt and a crooked composition.

A COUNTRY GARDEN *by Joanne Goldstein, 1998, Coral Springs, Florida, 43½ " x 43½ ". Because the appliqué design extends into the borders, I stitched the borders to the background before I completed the appliqué and embroidery.*

HELPFUL HINT

WHEN CUTTING A *small group of flowers, leaves, or petals, you don't have to cut out each motif individually. Cut a group of small images as one piece. Similarly, any leaves that are attached to flowers can remain attached and be cut as one piece. You may, however, choose to separate various parts of the motifs and rearrange them to better fit your design. The photo below shows two cutting options for the same group of fabric motifs.*

Preparing Theme-Fabric Motifs

Cut motifs from your theme fabric. Cut approximately ¼" beyond the edge of the printed design, eyeballing the distance and following the general shape of the motif. Try to simplify complicated shapes as you cut them out. It can be difficult to blanket-stitch around vines with delicate tendrils, fish with narrow fins, and trees with tiny branches. Simply cut off these details. Later, you can replace them with decorative stitches or beads.

Sometimes you may want to use large portions of your theme fabric without cutting it apart (see the Helpful Hint at left). Using small, sharp scissors, cut away the background part of the fabric, leaving the printed motif intact.

Finalizing the Design

Pin the large appliqué shapes and motifs in position on the background, then stand back and view your composition from a distance. Are the design elements in proportion to one another?

Pin theme fabrics in place to evaluate your design.

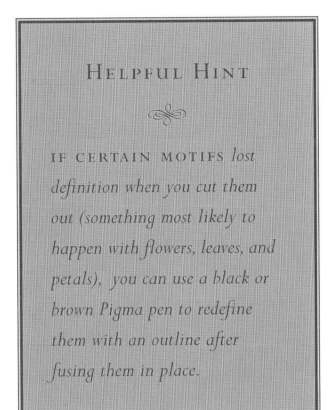
Do some areas of the design seem too busy and others too sparse? Have you included enough motifs to make your design interesting? Have you used too many motifs, making your design look cluttered? Have you achieved an overall pleasing composition?

Don't rush through this process. Make changes, move pieces around, check the arrangement in the mirror. Mirrors reflect a reversed image, and this different perspective can make it easier to spot design weaknesses.

You may want to leave the quilt hanging for a few days to make sure you are happy with your work. Trust your instincts and don't be afraid to make changes. When you are satisfied with the composition, make sure all the appliqués are pinned securely in place.

You will need to remove the motifs in order to attach fusible web to them and appliqué the

freezer-paper shapes. Take a picture of the design before you remove any appliqués. The photo will be a handy reference when it's time to put the pieces back on the quilt top.

Making Bias Strips

Since many floral and landscape quilts use bias strips for stems and branches, it's important that you know how to make these easy and versatile strips. My favorite method is to use bias bars. Start with ½ yard of fabric, and fold a corner diagonally so that the edges align as shown.

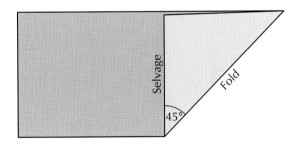

Lightly press the crease. Open the folded fabric and use a ruler and rotary cutter to cut 1"-wide bias strips parallel to the crease.

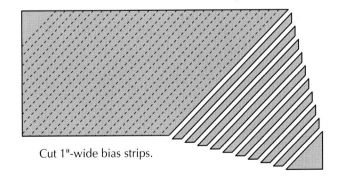

Cut 1"-wide bias strips.

Fold each bias strip in half lengthwise, wrong sides together. Stitch the strip to the desired width. For example, if the finished bias strip needs to be ¼" wide, stitch ¼" from the folded edge. Trim the seam allowance close to the stitching. Insert a ¼" bias bar into the resulting

CORNUCOPIA *by Joanne Goldstein, 1998, Coral Springs, Florida, 43½" x 47½".*
The placement of fabric motifs contributes to the illusion of perspective: large-scale vegetables in the foreground,
medium-scale leaves in the middleground, and small-scale trees and buildings in the background.

tube and turn the tube until the seam allowance falls along the center back of the bias bar. Press flat, then remove the bias bar and press again. You now have a perfectly stitched bias tube, ready to be appliquéd to a quilt.

APPLIQUÉING THE DESIGN

Before you begin to appliqué, decide whether you will include embellishments such as lace, doilies, or handkerchiefs. Position these items on your background, overlapping pieces as needed. Baste them in place.

Unpin the freezer-paper templates and prepare them for your favorite method of appliqué. There are a couple methods to consider: freezer-paper template on top of the fabric shape, or underneath it.

Freezer Paper on Top

To appliqué with the freezer-paper template on top, iron the template to the fabric with the shiny side facing the right side of the fabric. The paper will temporarily adhere to the fabric. Cut out the shape, leaving a scant ¼" of fabric beyond the freezer-paper template. Pin the template (with the fabric adhered to it) to the quilt top, with the paper facing up. When you appliqué the piece to the quilt, use your needle to turn under the seam allowance as you go, using the paper template as a turn-under guide.

Freezer Paper Underneath

For the template-underneath method, you'll need to reverse all the templates, or your finished design will be flopped. To reverse the templates, simply trace the pattern onto the shiny side of the freezer paper with a permanent marker (a pencil won't work). Cut out the template and iron it to the fabric with the shiny side facing the wrong side of the fabric. Cut out the shape, leaving a ¼" seam allowance. Position and pin the appliqués on the quilt top with the paper facing down, pinning through the paper. Turn the seam allowance under the edge of the paper as you appliqué.

After you've prepared all the pieces, thread a quilting needle with one strand of embroidery floss in a color that closely matches the appliqué fabric. Embroidery floss is so soft that it lets you achieve tiny, invisible hand appliqué stitches. Or if you prefer, you can machine appliqué these shapes in place using either a satin stitch or an invisible appliqué stitch.

Appliqué the pieces in place. Be careful not to stitch through the paper, or it will be difficult to remove. Appliqué only the design elements you drew on freezer paper. The theme-fabric motifs you cut will be appliquéd later.

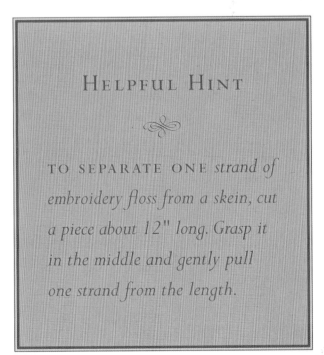

HELPFUL HINT

TO SEPARATE ONE *strand of embroidery floss from a skein, cut a piece about 12" long. Grasp it in the middle and gently pull one strand from the length.*

After the pieces are appliquéd, turn the quilt over and, using sharp scissors, carefully cut away the background behind the appliqués. Be careful not to cut into the front of the quilt top. Insert a pin into the background fabric and gently lift it to separate the background fabric from the appliqué. Slowly and carefully trim the excess fabric behind the appliqué, leaving a full ¼" seam allowance in the background fabric. Gently peel the freezer paper from the appliqué.

APPLYING FUSIBLE WEB TO MOTIFS

Once the large shapes are appliquéd to the quilt top, pin the theme-fabric motifs back in place. Remove the motifs one at a time (A), pinning the wrong side of each to the textured side (the glue side) of fusible web. Cut the shape from the web. Remove the pins.

Protect your ironing surface with a thick, folded towel. Lay the motif right side down on the towel, then place the textured side of

HELPFUL HINT

❧

ALWAYS ALLOW THE *fused fabric to cool completely before removing the paper backing. To easily remove the paper, gently score through it with a pin.*

the fusible web over it. Press the web to the motif, following the manufacturer's directions to ensure a secure bond (B). After the web is securely attached, trim along the edge of the motif (C). Carefully remove the paper backing (D), reposition the motif on the quilt, and pin it

Carefully cut away fabric behind the appliqués.

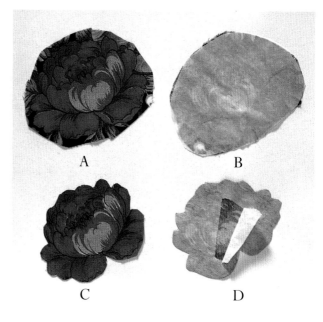

(A) Choose a fabric motif.
(B) Fuse web to back of motif.
(C) Cut along edge of motif.
(D) Remove paper backing.

in place. Continue this procedure until you've applied fusible web to all the motifs. *Don't* fuse the motifs to the quilt at this time.

With the various design elements appliquéd to the quilt and the motifs pinned in place, it's time to make final adjustments. Check your design in a mirror for balance, composition, and arrangement. Once you're absolutely certain that the design is complete, fuse the motifs to the background. Protect your ironing surface with a folded towel, then press the motifs in place, using a press cloth over the motifs to protect your iron. Check each motif to be sure it is securely fused to the quilt top.

A completed quilt top, ready for embroidery.

Embroidering Your Quilt

You can add texture and definition to your design with a variety of threads and embroidery stitches. The first step is to embroider the edge of each motif with a blanket stitch (which is sometimes referred to as a buttonhole stitch). The blanket stitch is versatile and easy to master. It gives fused motifs a smooth, finished edge and allows you to easily appliqué a wide variety of unusual shapes. Once you've blanket-stitched all the motifs, you can add details with other embroidery stitches. The last step is to embellish the quilt top with silk-ribbon embroidery and beading.

USING AN EMBROIDERY HOOP

You can begin embroidering your quilt in any area, but I prefer to start in the center and work my way out to the edges. Center the part of the quilt that you will be working on in an 8" embroidery hoop. The fabric should be taut, but be careful not to stretch or pull it out of shape. Complete all the embroidery in one section before moving to the next.

An embroidery hoop is essential to your stitching success. It's impossible to achieve flat, uniform embroidery without one. If embroidering in a hoop feels awkward at first, practice until you feel confident manipulating the hoop.

The time and effort you spend learning to embroider this way will be well worth the effort. Your stitches will be neat and even, and the design will remain flat and smooth.

After you've put a section of the quilt in the hoop, fold the rest of the quilt top in toward the hoop. Pin the sides in place with large safety pins. Your quilt edges will look like a window frame around the embroidery hoop. Folding the quilt around the hoop prevents the sides from stretching out of shape while you work. It also keeps the quilt top clean by preventing it from

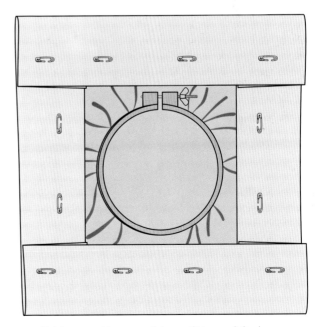

Fold top and bottom of the quilt toward the hoop
and pin with large safety pins.

Experiment with a variety of threads.

hanging down around your feet—or your pets—while you embroider. The section that you are working on will be clearly visible, and the rest of the top will be protected. After you've finished embroidering the section in your hoop, unpin and unfold the top, reposition the hoop, and refold.

EMBROIDERING THE MOTIFS

You can match the embroidery thread closely to the motifs or you can use contrasting thread. Try both methods in the same quilt.

Experiment with all sorts of threads for exciting—and sometimes surprising—results. Use metallic thread for sparkle, or separate metallic thread into one ply and use it with two strands of regular embroidery floss for a subtle shimmer. For low-key shine, try variegated embroidery floss, or rayon or silk threads. (Silk thread is very fine, so use four or more strands at once to make sure your efforts show!) If you want a heavy, well-defined look, use perle cotton.

If you use embroidery floss, use a size 7 or 8 Embroidery needle and keep extra needles on hand. Embroidering through multiple layers (the fused motif and the pieced background) can easily cause your needle to bend or even break, and the points will become dull. Replace bent or dull needles to ensure frustration-free stitching. Use two strands of floss in lengths of approximately 12". Longer pieces tangle easily and are more likely to wear thin and break.

THE BLANKET STITCH

Make a small knot at one end of the thread. Using the illustration below as a guide, bring your needle up at point A through the back of the quilt top at the edge of the fused piece. Insert the needle at point B and make a small straight stitch. Bring the needle up at point C, making sure the thread is under the tip of the needle. As you continue to add stitches, make sure the line formed along the top of the stitches lies along the edge of the fused motif. Take care to space your stitches evenly. The "bite" each stitch takes into the motif should be about the same length as the distance between each stitch. The bulkier your motifs and threads, the bigger your spacing can be. But try to make stitches about ⅛" long for starters and see how you like the look.

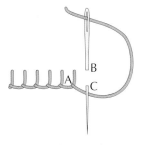

Blanket Stitch

When you've stitched all the way around the motif, bring the needle to the back of the quilt and end the stitching with a small knot close to the fabric. Weave the needle through the back of several stitches and cut off the tail.

Be sure to keep your stitches evenly spaced and uniform in size. If the motif changes color as you stitch around it, you may want to change the color of your thread to match.

Stitching Outside Points

When you blanket stitch, it's necessary to take an extra stitch at the top of outside points to keep them sharp and neat. Using the illustration below as a guide, take your last blanket stitch about ⅛" before the point. Insert the needle directly into the point and make a small straight stitch. Bring the needle up one or two threads away from this straight stitch, then complete another blanket stitch on the other side of the point.

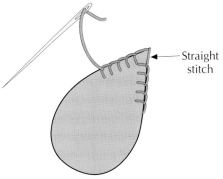

Straight stitch

Stitching Inside Points

Stitch inside points as shown below. Notice how the stitches splay apart at an inside corner—just the opposite of an outside point.

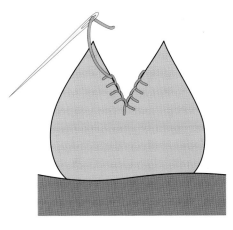

Stitching Curves

As you embroider around curves, keep the stitch length even.

Although many newer sewing machines have blanket-stitch capabilities, hand stitching offers a unique look that cannot be obtained with a machine. However, if you wish to experiment with machine blanket stitches, set the machine for a short stitch length and use a stabilizer under the fabric. Practice until your machine embroidery is neat and even. You will need to raise the presser foot and pivot often as you stitch around curves.

Whether you embroider by machine or by hand, try different types of thread to see the variety of effects you can obtain. When your practice stitches look neat and uniform, begin embroidering your quilt. Stitch completely

Confidence Builder 4

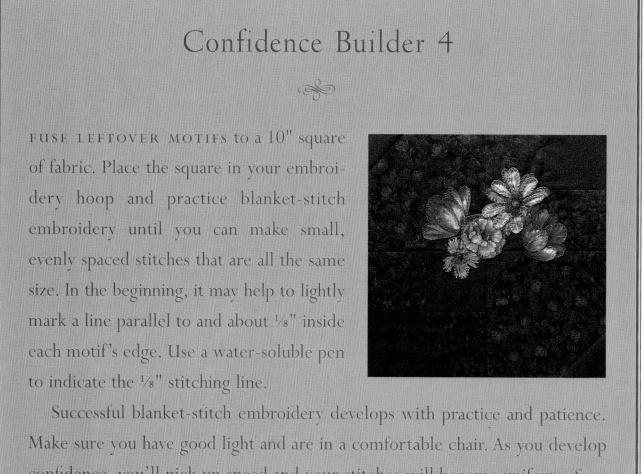

FUSE LEFTOVER MOTIFS to a 10" square of fabric. Place the square in your embroidery hoop and practice blanket-stitch embroidery until you can make small, evenly spaced stitches that are all the same size. In the beginning, it may help to lightly mark a line parallel to and about ⅛" inside each motif's edge. Use a water-soluble pen to indicate the ⅛" stitching line.

Successful blanket-stitch embroidery develops with practice and patience. Make sure you have good light and are in a comfortable chair. As you develop confidence, you'll pick up speed and your stitches will become uniform. Save this practice piece to use with Confidence Builder 5 (page 53).

around each motif. Where the motifs overlap, blanket-stitch around each one separately. Don't stitch around portions that are overlapped by another motif.

Blanket stitching defines each flower.

Continue embroidering until all the motifs are outlined with a blanket stitch. As you embroider and move your hoop around your quilt, you may notice that some of the fused pieces have become loose. Simply re-fuse them with a hot iron before stitching around them. Be sure to embroider each motif in place, but don't embroider around any of the large design elements you drew yourself. Blanket stitching emphasizes shapes, and you want the theme-fabric motifs—not a vase or other background element—to take center stage.

The blanket stitch has several variations, and you can use any of them to add variety to your quilt. You can even combine different stitches. Follow the diagrams below to practice these variations, then try them on your quilt. Experiment and let your imagination guide you!

Closed Blanket Stitch

Knotted Blanket Stitch

Crossed Blanket Stitch

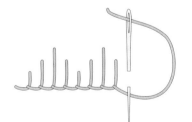

Pyramid Blanket Stitch

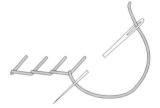

Slanted Blanket Stitch

Serpentine Blanket Stitch

Embellishing Your Quilt

EMBROIDERY STITCHES

I N ADDITION TO blanket stitching, you can embellish your quilt with a variety of other stitches. Enhance florals and landscapes with embroidered leaves, flowers, and branches. Add seaweed, tendrils, and marine fauna to seascapes. Embroider clouds, small animals, and insects in landscapes. Whatever the theme, now is your chance to add details that will make your quilt a visual and textural success.

Use a water-soluble marker, chalk marker, or pencil (mark lightly!) to indicate the placement of stems, branches, flowers, buds, leaves, clouds, or whatever you plan to embroider. The diagrams below show embroidery stitches that are easy to learn and effective on any quilt.

Remember, just as with the blanket stitch, you can use many kinds of thread. Don't limit yourself to embroidery floss.

Enhance your quilt with embroidery.

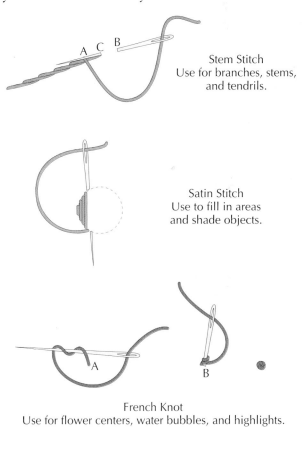

Stem Stitch
Use for branches, stems, and tendrils.

Satin Stitch
Use to fill in areas and shade objects.

French Knot
Use for flower centers, water bubbles, and highlights.

Backstitch
Use for small twigs, trailing lines, and outlines.

AUTUMN MOSAIC *by Joanne Goldstein, 1997, Coral Springs, Florida, 65" x 49½".*
Crazy quilting, appliqué, and embroidery balance beautifully in this rich seasonal design.
Notice how the background quilting near the tree trunks echoes the appliqué motifs.

SILK-RIBBON EMBROIDERY

It's easy—and quick—to add interest and texture to your quilt with silk-ribbon embroidery. Silk ribbon is available in 4mm, 7mm, and 13mm widths, and when you combine the range of sizes and colors with different stitches, the special effects you can create are just about limitless. Use 7mm ribbon to make leaves, flowers, and petals. The 4mm width is perfect for small French knots, buds, and accents. The wider 13mm ribbon makes it easy to add large leaves and flowers, as well as insects and butterflies.

Silk ribbon is delicate and frays easily, and the more you pull a ribbon through your quilt top, the more ragged it will become. To prevent fraying, or at least keep it to a minimum, cut short pieces (no longer than 12") to reduce wear. To thread ribbon through a needle, pierce the ribbon ¼" from its end, and pull the needle through to lock.

Threading the Needle

To make a knot, pierce the ribbon at points A and B as shown, then pull the needle through to form the knot.

Making a Knot

Use a Chenille needle for ribbon work. Use the diagrams on this page to practice stitches, keeping them loose and even.

The ribbon may tend to twist as you embroider. Try to keep it as straight and flat as possible. If the ribbon is twisted on the surface of your quilt, it won't show to its best advantage.

Feather Stitch
Bring needle up at A and down at B, leaving slack in stitch. Take a small stitch at C-D to form feather.

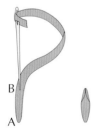

Japanese Ribbon Stitch
Insert needle at point B, then pull gently until ribbon curls at edges.

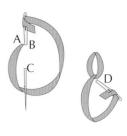

Lazy Daisy Stitch

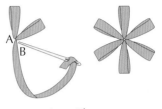

Loop Flower

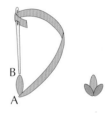

Rose Bud
Make a small straight stitch, then make a second stitch over the first to create a padded bud. Make 2 straight stitches at the bottom of the padded bud for leaves.

Spider Web Rose
Use one strand of floss to form spokes, then weave ribbon over and under until the spokes are covered.

INDIGO INFLUENCES *by Joanne Goldstein, 1998, Coral Springs, Florida, 50½" x 53".*
Embroidery, beads, and buttons fill out a stunning bouquet set against
a Grandmother's Flower Garden pieced background.

Add embroidery accents to theme motifs.

Embroidered vines and tendrils unify the design.

You can embroider directly over the fused motifs to highlight a particular area. For example, if your quilt features a floral design with roses, try embroidering silk-ribbon roses, rosebuds, and leaves directly over some of the fabric flowers and leaves.

Confidence Builder 5

❧

USING YOUR PRACTICE piece from Confidence Builder 4 (page 46), lightly draw lines with a water-soluble pen to indicate embroidery details. Insert the practice piece into your embroidery hoop. Using two strands of embroidery floss, embroider stems, branches, small flowers, and vines. Use silk ribbons to add small and large flowers, and leaves or grass. Remember to embroider directly over some of the printed motifs, not just in the background. With practice, embroidery will become easier and your details will be beautiful.

BEADS, BUTTONS, AND CHARMS

Use embellishments sparingly. You want the piecing, appliqué, and embroidery to be the focus of the quilt. Don't overwhelm and obscure the design with too many three-dimensional objects. Instead, use them to enhance what's already there. For example, use buttons as flower centers, or add pieces of lace to suggest a curtain or tablecloth. There are lots of creative ways to add decorative accents to your work. Just remember to keep them in proportion to the rest of the quilt.

Clustered seed beads add sparkle to flowers.

Beads

Beads add dimension and sparkle and are available in many shapes and sizes. Seed beads are round and make perfect flower centers, buds, tiny blooms, and dewdrops. A line of seed beads spilling out of a bouquet subtly suggests tendrils and ferns. Bugle beads, which are cylindrical, are perfect for indicating branches, twigs, and grass. Experiment with different sizes to see the effects they create. For a dramatic look, group beads in clusters.

Use a long, slender beading needle to attach beads. Most other needles won't fit through the small holes in the beads. Beading thread is also a necessity—don't skimp and use sewing thread. When you take the time to add glittering beads

to your quilt, you don't want to risk your thread breaking and your beads disappearing.

Make a small knot at the end of the thread. Center the quilt area you are working on in an embroidery hoop. Bring the needle up from the back of the quilt and slide a bead onto the needle. Take a tiny stitch. Continue adding beads in this way. After every four or five beads, make a knot in the thread at the back of the quilt close to the fabric. Do not cut the thread; just continue adding beads with a tiny stitch. Knotting at intervals will secure the beads and prevent an entire area from unraveling should any beads come loose.

Buttons, Charms, and More

You may have already added doilies, linens, lace, or other embellishments during the appliqué stage, but if you didn't, you might want to add something like that now. Buttons, pins, brass charms, and small pieces of costume jewelry can also make excellent accents, so look through your collections for hidden treasure. If you decide to include embellishments, stitch them securely to the quilt top with beading thread.

A colorful button bird perches on a branch.

"Floating" tendrils of yarn and ribbon add texture to this underwater scene, and a pink doily suggests delicate coral.

Finishing the Quilt

❧❦

Your APPLIQUÉD, embroidered, and embellished quilt top is beautiful. But let's face it; it's not a quilt until it's quilted and bound. Perhaps you want to add borders, or you may want to move right to quilting, binding, and attaching a hanging sleeve. Whatever your fancy, this section will help you turn your project into a completed work of art.

PRESSING

Carefully press the quilt top with a dry, warm (not hot) iron. Cover your ironing surface with a thickly folded towel so you won't flatten your quilt. Be especially careful when pressing near silk-ribbon embroidery—you don't want to squash the stitches as you press. Similarly, be careful around beadwork and other embellishments. You don't want to crush any three-dimensional features or snag the iron on beads, buttons, or other attachments.

After pressing, make sure all four sides of the quilt are straight and even, since they may have distorted slightly due to the embroidery. Before adding borders or layering and basting, square up the corners and straighten the sides, if necessary, with your rotary cutter and ruler.

BORDERS

Borders frame the quilt and give it a finished look. However, many quilts can stand on their own without borders. This is especially true of contemporary designs.

The border colors should complement the quilt top, and the size should be in proportion to the rest of the quilt. On quilts that measure between 50" and 60", a 4" border gives a neat, framed finish. Attaching a narrow inner border (1" to 1½" wide) is like adding a mat to a painting before it's framed.

On heavily appliquéd, embroidered, and embellished quilts, a simple border is usually the most effective. An elaborately pieced border would compete with the rest of the quilt top. If the border seems overly plain, let some small appliquéd and embroidered motifs spill over from the quilt onto the border for a more unified look.

You can opt for either mitered or straight-cut corners. Miters make the border look more like a picture frame, but both styles have their places. If you're uncertain about what style suits your quilt, browse through the quilts shown in this book to see which style you like best.

Measuring for Borders

To keep your quilt square, it's critical that you measure the quilt top before you add the borders. Measure the quilt top through the center in each direction—width and length—don't measure along the edges. If you're adding multiple borders, measure after each addition.

For straight-cut borders, measure the quilt top and cut borders to fit two opposite sides of the quilt. After attaching these borders, measure the quilt top again, including the borders you just added, then cut the next two borders to that measurement. Don't stitch longer border sections to the quilt top and trim later. This would only make it easier for your quilt to stretch out of shape.

For mitered borders, you need to cut strips longer than the quilt sides. Measure the quilt top through the center to determine the quilt-top dimensions, then add two times the width of your borders plus 4" to that measurement. Cut your border strip to that length. If you're adding multiple borders, you can stitch all the borders for one side of the quilt together before adding them to the quilt top. Fold the borders in half to find the center and mark with a pin. Match the border's center to the center edge of the quilt top. Pin the border to the quilt top and stitch, starting and stopping ¼" from each end of the quilt. Repeat for all four sides of the quilt.

At the ironing board, fold back one end of a border at a 45° angle, and press. Pin in place. At the sewing machine, open the fold and sew the borders together, stitching in the crease.

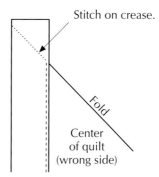

Stitch on crease.

Fold

Center of quilt (wrong side)

Stitch all four corners in the same manner. Trim the excess fabric, leaving a ¼" seam allowance. Press the seam allowances open.

BATTING

Choose a thin, flat batting for your quilt. Wall quilts should lie flat, and puffiness will detract from the dimensional effects you stitched into the surface. In addition, if you plan to hand quilt, remember that some portions of the quilt (the fused motifs) consist of multiple layers. The thinner the batting, the easier it will be to quilt through. Consider separating a low-loft batting into two layers for a very soft, thin, and easy-to-quilt "sandwich." Lightweight fleece, which is sold by the yard, is also an excellent choice.

LAYERING AND BASTING

If your quilt is larger than 40" in both directions, you'll need to piece the backing fabric. Purchase enough fabric for two lengths of the quilt. Cut the fabric in half, trim the selvages, then sew the two pieces together side by side. Press the seams open for easier quilting. Trim the pieced backing so it's approximately 3" larger than your quilt top. Save the excess fabric to make a hanging sleeve.

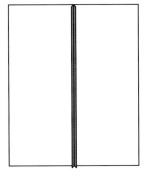

For large quilt backings,
sew fabric lengths together.

Lay the backing fabric on the floor or table, right side *down*. Place the batting over the backing, then add the quilt top, right side up. Baste the three layers together securely with white thread or with safety pins.

QUILTING

Begin quilting in the center of the quilt top on one of the printed motifs. Quilt on and around the motif, following the design on the fabric.

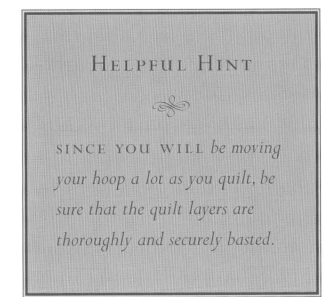

HELPFUL HINT

❧

SINCE YOU WILL *be moving your hoop a lot as you quilt, be sure that the quilt layers are thoroughly and securely basted.*

For example, if the motif is a flower with leaves, quilt on the lines that indicate the petals and leaf veins. Add quilting accents to all the motifs. As you quilt, you will notice that the design becomes much more three-dimensional.

You can finish your quilt with either machine or hand quilting—or try a combination of both. If you choose to machine quilt, consider hand quilting the motif sections and

Quilt inside motifs to highlight contours.

Quilt leaves to add dimension.

COASTAL SUNSET *by Joanne Goldstein, 1998, Coral Springs, Florida, 54" x 45".*
A quilted diagonal grid in the first border contrasts perfectly with the horizontal lines
and gentle curves in the strip-pieced background.

machine quilting the background. If you decide to machine quilt the entire quilt, use free-motion quilting so that you can move easily around the design. Be careful to avoid quilting over any embellishments.

Once all the motifs are quilted, move on to the pieced background. Simple quilting, such as grids, diagonal lines, and in-the-ditch stitching are usually most effective. Simple, traditional quilting in the background enhances the more complex quilting and embellishing in the appliqué design.

When all the quilting is completed, trim the batting and backing fabric so they are even with the quilt top. Once again, check that the quilt is square and hasn't distorted during quilting. If it has, square up the quilt as needed.

ADDING A HANGING SLEEVE

Using leftovers from the quilt backing, cut a piece of fabric 8½" wide by the width of your quilt. Turn the short edges under ¼", then turn them under again. Stitch the fold in place to hem the edges. Fold the fabric in half so that the long, raw edges meet. Press. Pin or machine baste the hanging sleeve to the back of the quilt, aligning the raw edges of the sleeve with the raw edges of the top of the quilt. The raw edges will be enclosed in the binding.

Hand sew the folded edge of the sleeve to the quilt back with a blindstitch. Stitch through the backing and batting for extra security.

BINDING THE EDGES

Cut enough binding strips to go around the perimeter of your quilt, adding about 5" extra for mitering the corners. You can cut strips anywhere from 2" to 2¼" wide.

Stitch the binding strips together end to end with diagonal seams to make one continuous strip. Fold the strip in half lengthwise and press. Using a ¼" seam allowance, stitch the folded strip to the right side of the quilt top using a walking foot.

To miter the corners, stop stitching ¼" from the corner. Clip the threads and fold the binding at a 45° angle.

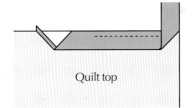

Quilt top

Fold the binding back down, flush with the edge of the quilt as shown. Begin stitching the binding to the next side of the quilt. Repeat for each corner. When you reach the starting point, overlap the ends of the binding and stitch in place. Fold the binding to the back of the quilt and hand stitch in place.

Quilt top

Frequently Asked Questions

⚜

THE FOLLOWING QUESTIONS are the ones quilters ask me most often. The answers will help you plan dramatic quilts and solve problems you may encounter along the way.

How do I know what kind of fabric is suitable to use as theme fabric?

Any fabric with well-defined motifs or pictures can be used as a theme fabric. Look for colorful florals, animals, fish, and insects. There is probably a theme fabric suitable for almost any design you can think of. In addition to quilting cottons, many home-decorating fabrics provide colorful, large-scale motifs, such as cabbage roses, garden latticework, barnyard animals, and underwater creatures.

Why doesn't my design show up well against the pieced background?

If your design disappears against the pieced background, there probably isn't enough contrast between the background (your canvas) and the motifs. You can use a dark, medium, or light background—your choice should depend on the value of the motifs you plan to use. Bright florals will shine against a dark background, as in "Floral Elegance" on page 69, but they would disappear against a similarly bright background.

If the pieced pattern you've chosen for your background is complicated, it will probably compete with the rest of the quilt for attention. Aim for a simple, subtle background.

Do I have to use 100% cotton fabric?

Absolutely not! Stick to 100% cotton fabric for the pieced background, but feel free to experiment with all types of fabric for the appliqué design. Since you will fuse the motifs to the background, you can use almost any type of fabric, including silk, satin, rayon, and blends. Be sure to stop at the decorator-fabric counter for a great selection of unusual and interesting design choices.

How can I prevent the fused motifs from falling off while I embroider the quilt?

Due to the constant handling and repositioning of the embroidery hoop, you may find that some of the fused motifs come loose. Simply pin them back in place and fuse them again. Remember to fold your quilt into a "quilt window" (page 43) to protect it from unnecessary handling. It sometimes helps to pin the fused motifs with tiny sequin pins. The tiny pins do not get in the way of stitching and will keep the motifs from falling off the quilt.

FLORAL TAPESTRY *by Joanne Goldstein, 1998, Coral Springs, Florida, 49" x 41½".*

Large flowers, cut from decorator fabrics, fill the foreground. Medium and dark greens give the lower pieced background depth.

How can I keep my embroidery needle from bending or breaking?

If your needle bends or breaks while you are embroidering, it is probably too small. The higher the size number, the smaller and thinner the needle. If you're using a size 8 Embroidery needle, try switching to a size 7. The slightly thicker needle will easily accommodate embroidery floss, perle cotton, and rayon thread. Keep several needles on hand, since some bending is unavoidable. And all needles eventually wear and become dull, so change your needle periodically, regardless of bending.

Can I use machine embroidery?

If your machine has a blanket-stitch setting, you can use it to embroider the motifs. Use a short stitch length and practice until you can make even stitches. Change the top thread to match or contrast with each motif as desired. And take this opportunity to experiment with all the wonderful machine-embroidery threads that are available. Machine quilting threads work well for blanket stitching, too.

Why does my silk-ribbon embroidery look messy and uneven?

To achieve beautiful silk-ribbon embroidery, keep the ribbon length to about 12". The delicate silk frays easily, and using a short ribbon lessens the wear. Also, it's important to keep your stitches loose. Silk-ribbon embroidery is easy to master with a little practice.

Will it be difficult to quilt through so many layers?

To make hand quilting through multiple layers easier, it's very important that you cut away the background fabric behind appliqués. When you are quilting within the fused motifs, use a slightly larger quilting needle (size 8 works well), and take no more than two or three stitches on the needle at a time.

Can I machine quilt an embellished fabric-collage quilt?

Of course! Lower the feed dogs and free-motion quilt the motifs so you can move easily around the design. Quilt the appliqué motifs first, then quilt a simple design in the background patchwork.

These quilts look complicated, and I'm a beginning quilter. Will I be successful?

Absolutely. You'll be amazed at how easy it is to make wonderful, unique designs. Using printed fabric motifs makes it easy to impart realism and variety to your quilts. If you've completed one pieced quilt and one appliqué quilt, you have all the necessary skills. Don't be afraid to experiment with new fabrics and take design risks. That's what creating art is all about!

Projects

❦

ON THE FOLLOWING pages you'll find complete directions for three quilts. Start with the easy and dramatic "Floral Elegance" on page 69. Completing this quilt will make you a master of the techniques discussed in this book. Your quilt will probably look completely different from the sample because of the theme fabrics you choose—remember that you are the artist. Through your fabric choices, you'll be expressing your unique sense of color and design. Trust yourself and your collage quilt will be a success.

Once you feel comfortable with the techniques you've learned, you'll be ready for "Tea Time" on page 77. This quilt has a traditional pieced background, several appliqué additions, and a detailed motif design, so it's a bit more challenging.

Once you've developed both skills and confidence, it's time to design your own quilt. The directions provided for "Shangri-La" on page 87 will help you get started on a spectacular landscape. Make the quilt as shown, or use it as a starting point for your own creation.

Floral Elegance

FLORAL ELEGANCE *by Joanne Goldstein, 1998, Coral Springs, Florida, 45" x 45".*

SIMPLE PIECING combines with elegant embroidery and embellishments to make this quilt a knockout! But don't let the stunning results worry you—it's easy to make. Remember though, your quilt will look different from the one in the photograph simply because your theme fabrics will be different. Use the directions as a guide to making a unique work of art.

MATERIALS

NOTE: *All fabrics are 100% cotton quilting fabrics, unless otherwise specified. All measurements are based on 42"-wide fabrics.*

- 2¼ yds. black solid for center square, borders, and binding
- ⅝ yd. black print for corner triangles
- ⅜ yd. print for narrow borders
- ½ yd. green
- ½ yd. gold satin taffeta
- 1½ yds. *total* (approximately) of various theme fabrics with small, medium, and large flowers
- Scrap of butterfly fabric, enough to yield two butterflies
- 2⅔ yds. fabric for backing
- 2 yds. fusible web
- Low-loft batting, approximately 48" x 48"

EMBELLISHING SUPPLIES

- Embroidery floss, perle cotton, and decorative threads in assorted colors
- Embroidery and Chenille needles in various sizes
- Buttons for flowers
- Silk ribbon in assorted colors and widths for flowers and leaves
- Beads of assorted sizes, colors, and styles
- Beading needle
- Beading thread

CUTTING FOR BACKGROUND

NOTE: *Please read all the directions before beginning, so you'll be familiar with the techniques used.*

From the black solid, cut:
- 1 square, 20½" x 20½"

From the lengthwise grain of the remaining black solid, cut:
- 2 strips, each 1½" x 29" (A)
- 2 strips, each 1½" x 31" (B)
- 2 strips, each 2½" x 32" (E)
- 2 strips, each 2½" x 36" (F)
- 2 strips, each 4½" x 37" (I)
- 2 strips, each 4½" x 45" (J)

From the black print, cut:
- 2 squares, each 16" x 16"; cut each square in half diagonally to make 4 half-square triangles

From the print for narrow borders, cut:
- 2 strips, each 1" x 31" (C)
- 2 strips, each 1" x 32" (D)
- 2 strips, each 1" x 36" (G)
- 2 strips, each 1" x 37" (H)

PIECING THE BACKGROUND

1. Sew black print triangles to 2 opposite sides of the 20½" black square. The triangles will be slightly oversized. Press the seam allowances toward the square, then attach the remaining 2 triangles and press again. Trim the edges ¼" from the points of the square so the resulting square measures 29" x 29".

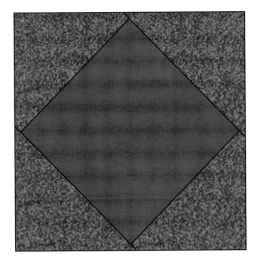

2. Sew the black solid A strips to the sides of the pieced square; press the seam allowances toward the border strips. Sew the B strips to the top and bottom edges; press.

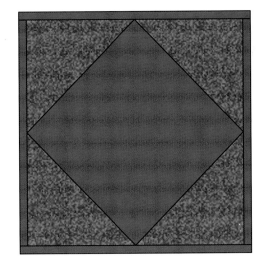

3. Add the C–J strips in the same manner, adding the side borders first, pressing, then adding the top and bottom borders and pressing again.

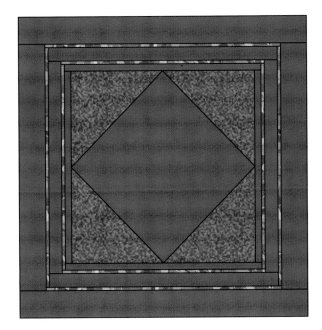

APPLIQUÉING THE STEMS AND BOW

1. From the green fabric, cut 12 bias strips, each 1" wide. The strips will vary in length from 20" to 30" long. Use the strips to make ¼"-wide bias tubes (page 37). Using the illustration below as a guide, appliqué the bias tubes to the quilt top.

2. From the gold taffeta, cut 3 bias strips, each 1½" x 20". Use the strips to make ½"-wide bias tubes. Appliqué the bias tubes to the quilt top in the form of a bow.

FUSING THE FLOWERS

1. From the theme fabrics, cut out small, medium, and large flowers. When cutting, follow the general shape of the motif, leaving an approximate ¼"-wide seam allowance. Continue to cut out flowers, leaves, and buds. Be sure to include motifs of various sizes.

2. Pin flowers, leaves, and buds to the quilt to form a lush bouquet. Follow the general arrangement shown in the quilt photo. Remember, your arrangement will look different because your motifs will be different.

3. One at a time, remove the motifs and iron them to the textured side of fusible web. Follow the manufacturer's instructions to ensure the best possible bond. After the fusible web has cooled, cut each fused motif along its outline. Score the paper backing with a pin and peel it off. Pin the motif back in place on the quilt top.

4. From the butterfly fabric, cut 2 butterfly motifs, leaving an approximate ¼"-wide seam allowance. Iron the butterflies to the fusible web, cut along the outlines, and then pin them to the quilt top.

5. Cut out several additional flower, leaf, and bud motifs. Arrange them in one corner of the quilt, extending the arrangement into the borders. When you are satisfied with the corner arrangement, cut out and arrange similar motifs in each of the other corners.

6. Fuse the motifs in place. Use a press cloth, and don't forget to remove the pins before you press.

EMBROIDERING AND EMBELLISHING

1. Using embroidery floss, perle cotton, or decorative thread, blanket-stitch around each motif (pages 45–47). Follow the outline of the motif and make sure your stitches cover the edge. Use a variety of threads, and try changing colors with each motif.

2. Add other embroidery details to the motifs. I used various threads and colors to enhance every flower, leaf, and butterfly.

HELPFUL HINT

YOU CAN CHANGE *threads right in the middle of a motif. Notice how I switched from light blue floss on the light petals to heavier and darker perle cotton on the dark petals.*

3. Using outline and running stitches in embroidery floss or perle cotton, embroider cascading vines and tendrils among the flowers. Consider using a feather stitch to add light-colored branches.

4. Using an outline stitch in embroidery floss or perle cotton, embroider a vine, winding it through the appliquéd bow.

5. Stitch silk-ribbon leaves, flowers, and buds (see page 51 for stitches). Add small leaves to the vine that winds through the bow.

6. Stitch beads to flower centers or to other areas you want to highlight.

7. Sew any decorative buttons you've chosen to the quilt top. I used small flower buttons for my quilt.

QUILTING AND FINISHING

1. Cut the backing fabric into 2 pieces, each 1⅓ yards (48") long. Trim the selvages, then stitch the pieces together. If you plan to quilt by hand, press the seam open to reduce bulk; if you plan to machine quilt, press the seam to one side. Trim the backing to approximately 48" x 48".

2. Layer the backing, batting, and quilt top, then baste them together.

3. Following the design lines on the printed motifs, quilt the flower petals, leaves, and butterflies.

4. Quilt diagonal lines in the corner triangles of the center block, and cables in the border.

5. From the black solid, cut 5 strips for your binding. Depending on the thickness of your batting, you may want to cut them 2" or 2¼" wide. Following the directions on page 61, sew the binding to your quilt.

6. Referring to "Adding a Hanging Sleeve" on page 61, make a sleeve and attach it to the back of your quilt.

7. Sign and date your work of art.

Tea Time

TEA TIME *by Joanne Goldstein, 1998, Coral Springs, Florida, 67" x 62".*

THIS CHARMING quilt consists of a simple pieced background, easy appliqué, and an abundance of pansy and berry motifs. When choosing theme fabrics for your quilt, consider roses, daffodils, daisies, tulips, or any flower that you love. In addition, you could easily substitute clusters of grapes, cherries, apples, or other delicious fruits for the strawberries.

FINISHED BLOCK SIZE: 7½"

BLOCKS NEEDED: 18 plain blocks, 17 pieced blocks

MATERIALS

NOTE: *All fabrics are 100% cotton quilting fabrics, unless otherwise specified. All measurements are based on 42"-wide fabrics.*

- 1 yd. light yellow print
- ⅝ yd. medium yellow floral
- ⅝ yd. medium yellow print
- 1⅝ yds. floral print for tablecloth
- 1 yd. white for teapot, cup, saucer, plate, and sugar bowl
- ⅝ yd. brown print for basket
- ½ yd. brown solid for basket trim
- ½ yd. light brown for hanging basket
- ¾ yd. green print for flower stems and vines
- ½ yd. dark floral print for inner border
- 2 yds. gold print for outer border and binding
- 6" x 10" scrap of small-scale floral print for small pitcher
- 2" x 2" scrap of white for drop of cream
- 4 yds. fabric for backing
- 2½ yds. fusible web
- Low-loft batting, approximately 65" x 70"

THEME FABRICS

- 1 yd. (approximately) pansy or other floral print (use a print that includes flowers of several different sizes)
- ½ yd. (approximately) very small-scale floral print for decorative details on tea set
- 1 yd. (approximately) strawberry print (enough to yield about 50 strawberries), or fruit fabric of your choice
- ⅛ yd. (approximately) lemon print (enough to yield 12 lemons)

EMBELLISHING SUPPLIES

- Embroidery floss, perle cotton, and decorative threads in assorted colors
- 1 skein gold metallic floss
- Embroidery and Chenille needles in various sizes
- 10" doily
- 1 lace-trimmed napkin
- Buttons for flowers
- Silk ribbon in assorted colors and widths for flowers and leaves
- Beads of assorted sizes, colors, and styles
- Beading needle
- Beading thread

CUTTING FOR BACKGROUND

From the light yellow print, cut:
- 4 strips, each 8" x 42"; cut the strips into 18 squares, each 8" x 8" (A)

From the medium yellow floral, cut:
- 4 strips, each 2¼" x 42" (B)
- 2 strips, each 4½" x 42" (C)

From the medium yellow print, cut:
- 4 strips, each 2¼" x 42" (D)
- 2 strips, each 4½" x 42" (E)

From the *lengthwise* grain of the floral print for the tablecloth, cut:
- 1 strip, 10½" x 54" (F)

PIECING THE BACKGROUND

1. Sew a floral strip (B) to either side of a medium yellow print strip (E) as shown below. Make 2 strip sets.

2. Cut the strip sets crosswise into 34 segments, each 2¼" wide.

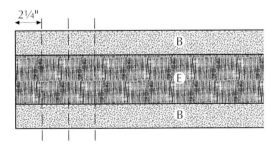

3. Sew a medium yellow print strip (D) to either side of a medium yellow floral strip (C). Make 2 of these strip sets.

4. Cut the strip sets crosswise into 17 segments, each 4½" wide.

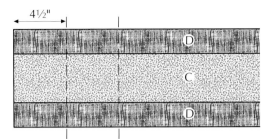

5. Sew a 2¼" segment to either side of a 4½" segment to make a pieced block. Repeat to make 17 pieced blocks.

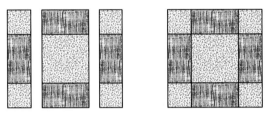

6. Lay out the blocks, alternating plain squares with the pieced blocks, to make 5 rows of 7 blocks. Sew the blocks into rows, pressing the seam allowances open. Sew the rows together. Press.

7. Sew the tablecloth fabric strip (F) to the bottom of the pieced unit. Press the seam allowance open.

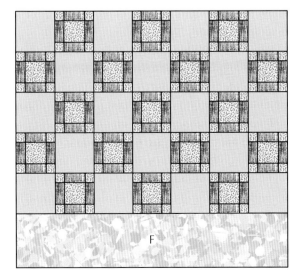

APPLIQUÉING THE
BASKETS AND TEA SET

1. Using the templates on the pullout, trace the appliqué shapes onto the dull side of freezer paper. Cut out the templates on the drawn lines. (The templates are reversed so you can iron the freezer-paper templates to the wrong side of the fabric. If you prefer to use freezer paper on top, reverse the templates before tracing.)

2. Iron the freezer-paper templates onto their corresponding fabrics. Cut out the appliqués, leaving a ¼" seam allowance beyond the edge of the freezer paper.

3. Pin the appliqués to the background.

4. From the brown solid, cut seven 1"-wide bias strips. Use the strips to make ½"-wide bias tubes. Appliqué the bias tubes to the basket (piece A) to indicate woven wicker.

5. Appliqué pieces A–R to the background in alphabetical order. The cream pitcher (piece S) will be added later. After appliquéing each

piece, turn the quilt over and carefully cut away the background behind the appliqué, leaving a full ¼" seam allowance. Remove the freezer paper.

6. Cut the doily in half. Turn under the cut edge of one half and appliqué it below the cream pitcher (S). Appliqué the pitcher and handle (T) in place. Appliqué the remaining doily half on top of the plate (N), again turning under the cut edge as you stitch.

7. Cut 3 bias strips, each 1¼" x 13", from the light brown fabric for the hanging basket. Appliqué the strips, then the hanging basket (U) in place, leaving the top edge open so you can insert stems later.

8. From the green print, cut fifteen 1"-wide bias strips. Use the strips to make ¼"-wide bias tubes of varying lengths. Appliqué the bias tubes around the woven and hanging baskets, referring to the photo on page 77 for placement. After the stems are in place, appliqué the tops of the baskets.

9. Cut a quarter-section from the lace-trimmed napkin as shown. Fold under the cut edges and appliqué the napkin next to the cup and saucer.

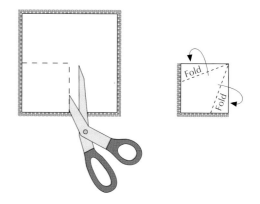

FUSING THE FRUITS AND FLOWERS

1. Cut flower and leaf motifs of various sizes from your theme fabrics. When cutting, follow the general shape of the motif, leaving about a ¼" seam allowance. Pin the flowers around the wicker basket, allowing some of them to spill over the top and down the sides. Don't skimp on the flowers. Use as many as needed to completely fill the basket with a lush bouquet.

2. Cut out tiny flower and leaf motifs and arrange them on the cup, saucer, teapot, plate, and sugar bowl to indicate decorative details. To make the pottery items look like a set, cut the same motifs for each piece.

3. Cut out small flowers and use them to decorate the edge of the napkin.

4. Cut out strawberries, leaves, and small flowers from your theme fabric. Fill the hanging basket with the motifs, allowing the berries to spill out and down the side of the basket.

5. One by one, remove the motifs and iron them to the textured side of fusible web. Follow the manufacturer's instructions to ensure the best possible bond. After the fusible web has cooled, cut out the fused motif along its outline. Score the paper backing with a pin and peel it off. Pin the motif in place on the quilt top.

6. Fuse the motifs in place. Use a press cloth, and don't forget to remove the pins before you press.

7. Once the baskets are filled, continue cutting out motifs and fusing them to other areas. Fill the plate with strawberries and place lemons near the teapot and on the saucer.

8. Fuse the drop of cream (V) below the spout of the small cream pitcher.

EMBROIDERING AND EMBELLISHING

1. Using embroidery floss, perle cotton, or decorative thread, blanket-stitch around each motif (pages 45–47). Follow the outline of the motif and make sure that your stitches cover the edge. Use a variety of thread types and colors. Use only 1 strand of floss when embroidering around tiny flowers.

2. Use other embroidery stitches in various threads and colors to add detail and dimension to each flower and berry.

3. Using 2 strands of gold metallic embroidery floss, make an outline stitch to indicate gold accents on the cup rim, handle, and saucer; teapot lid, top, and spout; and sugar-bowl top, handles, and plate.

4. Add tendrils to the flowers and berries with an outline or running stitch.

5. Fill out the bouquets in the baskets with silk-ribbon leaves, flowers, and buds.

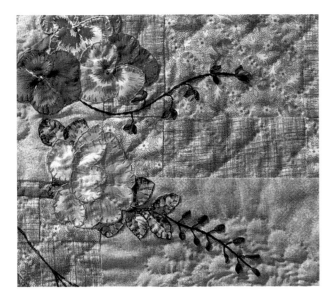

6. Add silk-ribbon accents to the doily under the pitcher.

7. Stitch beads to the berries and flowers. You might use seed beads to indicate seeds on the strawberries and bright stamens in the pansy centers.

8. Sew any buttons you've chosen to the quilt top. I added strawberry and flower buttons to my quilt, but you don't need to limit yourself to just the motifs that already appear in the quilt.

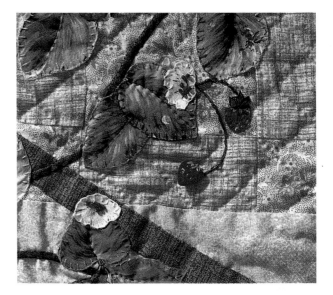

ADDING THE MITERED BORDERS

1. Measure the length and width of your quilt through the center. It should be approximately 53" x 48", but depending on how much stitching you did, your measurements may be a bit different. Square up the quilt top as needed (page 58).

2. From the dark floral print, cut 6 strips, each 2" x 42". Piece 3 strips together end to end, then cut the resulting long strip in half to make 2 long inner border strips. Repeat with the 3 remaining strips. Set the inner border strips aside.

3. From the lengthwise grain of the gold print, cut 4 strips, each 6" wide.

4. Sew 1 floral strip to each gold strip. Your strips will be longer than the edges of your quilt, but you'll need the excess fabric for mitering the corners.

5. Fold the border strips in half and mark the center of each with a pin. Match the center of a border to the center of the top edge of your quilt. Pin the gold edge of the border to the quilt top and stitch in place, starting and stopping ¼" from the edges of the quilt top. Don't trim the excess fabric. Repeat for each border.

6. Referring to "Borders" on page 57, miter all 4 corners. Press the seam allowances open.

7. From the green print, cut a 1" x 42" bias strip. You may need to piece 2 or 3 strips together to achieve the needed length. Appliqué the bias strips to the upper left and lower right corners of the borders.

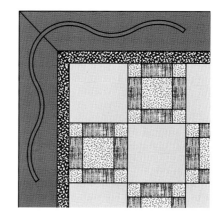

8. Cut out additional flower and fruit motifs and arrange them along the vine. Fuse the motifs in place and blanket-stitch the edges. Add embellishing touches with silk-ribbon embroidery and beads.

QUILTING AND FINISHING

1. Cut the backing fabric into 2 pieces, each 2 yards long. Trim the selvages, then stitch the pieces together. If you plan to quilt by hand, press the seam open to reduce bulk; if you plan to machine quilt, press the seam to one side. Trim the backing to approximately 65" x 70".

2. Layer the backing, batting, and quilt top, then baste them together.

3. Using the design lines on the motifs as guides, quilt the flower petals, leaves, lemons, and strawberries.

4. Quilt the wicker basket and pieced background. I quilted a 1" grid in the pieced blocks and a feathered wreath design in the plain blocks.

5. Quilt the borders as desired. My quilt has straight lines quilted parallel to the border.

6. Cut 7 strips of gold print for your binding. Depending on the thickness of your batting, you may want to cut them 2" or 2¼" wide. Following the directions in "Binding the Edges" on page 61, sew double-fold binding to your quilt.

7. Referring to "Adding a Hanging Sleeve" on page 61, make a sleeve and attach it to the back of your quilt.

8. Sign and date your work of art.

Shangri-La

SHANGRI-LA *by Joanne Goldstein, 1998, Coral Springs, Florida, 57" x 59".*

CREATE A landscape design on a sparkling background of small Nine Patch blocks. I've provided templates for four trees and instructions for appliquéing the bridge. The rest of the design is up to you! Choose a variety of theme fabrics for the landscape details, from birds in flight to majestic mountains. When you make the choices about which flora and fauna to include, your quilt becomes one-of-a-kind and expresses your personality.

FINISHED BLOCK SIZE: 3"

BLOCKS NEEDED: 195

MATERIALS

NOTE: *All fabrics are 100% cotton quilting fabrics, unless otherwise specified. All measurements are based on 42"-wide fabrics.*

- ⅛ yd. *each* of 2 different light yellows for horizon
- ⅛ yd. *each* of 2 different light purples for horizon
- ¼ yd. *each* of 3 different light blues for sky
- ¼ yd. *each* of 3 different light purples for sky
- ¼ yd. *each* of 3 different light yellows for sunrise
- ¼ yd. *each* of 3 different light peaches for sunrise
- ¼ yd. *each* of 3 different medium blues for water
- ¼ yd. *each* of 3 different medium purples for water

- ⅜ yd. *each* of 6 different medium greens for grass
- ½ yd. brown #1 for bridge
- 1 yd. brown #2 for trees
- ½ yd. light purple for inner border
- ⅜ yd. white for middle border
- 1⅜ yds. dark purple for outer border and binding
- Scraps of assorted greens for bias stems (each at least 10" square)
- 3½ yds. fabric for backing
- 2 yds. fusible web
- Low-loft batting, approximately 60" x 62"

THEME FABRICS

Collect a variety of theme fabrics so you can add the details your landscape needs. Look for trees, birds, rocks, flowers, insects, fish, grass, and mountains. You may even be able to find a great waterfall print. To give your design interest and depth, choose motifs that vary in size and color. The amount of fabric you need will depend on the size of the motifs. Refer to "Yardage for Theme Fabrics" on pages 24–25 for yardage suggestions.

EMBELLISHING SUPPLIES

- Embroidery floss, perle cotton, and decorative threads in assorted colors
- Embroidery and Chenille needles in various sizes
- Silk ribbon in assorted colors and widths for flowers and leaves
- Beads of assorted sizes, colors, and styles
- Beading needle
- Buttons

CUTTING FOR BACKGROUND

From *each* light yellow fabric for the horizon, cut:

- 1 strip, each 1½" x 42"

From *each* light purple fabric for the horizon, cut:

- 1 strip, each 1½" x 42"

From *each* fabric for the sky, sunrise, and water, cut:

- 3 strips, each 1½" x 42", for a total of 72 strips

From *each* medium green fabric for grass, cut:

- 6 strips, each 1½" x 42", for a total of 36 strips

PIECING THE BACKGROUND

1. Sew a light blue sky strip to either side of a light purple sky strip as shown. Cut the strip set into 1½"-wide segments. You'll need 27 segments.

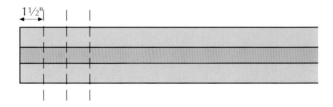

2. Reverse the color order and join the remaining light blue and light purple strips as shown. Cut the strip set into 1½"-wide segments. You'll need 27 segments.

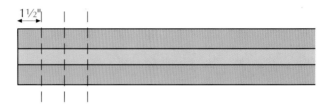

3. Sew the segments into Nine Patch blocks as shown. Make 18 blocks.

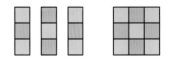

4. Repeat steps 1–3 to make 45 blue-and-purple Nine Patch blocks for the sky.

5. Repeat steps 1–3 with light yellow and peach strips to make 30 yellow-and-peach blocks for the sunrise.

6. Repeat steps 1–3 with medium blue and purple strips to make 45 Nine Patch blocks for the water.

7. Repeat steps 1–3 with medium green strips to make 75 Nine Patch blocks for the grass.

8. Using the illustration below as a guide, arrange the sky and sunrise Nine Patch blocks in 5 rows of 15 blocks each. Sew the blocks into rows, then join the rows.

9. Sew the 4 yellow-and-purple horizon strips together as shown below. Sew the strip set to the sky blocks.

10. Arrange the grass and water Nine Patch blocks in 8 rows of 15 blocks each. Sew the blocks into rows, then join the rows. Sew the block section to the horizon strips.

APPLIQUÉING THE BRIDGE AND TREES

1. From brown #1, cut 3 bias strips, each 1" x 20". Use the strips to make ¼"-wide bias tubes. Cut another 1"-wide brown bias strip, finish to ¼" wide, and cut it into five 2¼"-long segments. Referring to the photo on page 87 for placement, appliqué the bias strips to the middle of the horizon section. Appliqué the short strips first, then the long strips.

2. Using the templates on the pullout, trace the trees onto the dull side of freezer paper. (The templates are reversed, so if you appliqué with freezer paper on top, you'll have to reverse the templates.) Cut out the templates on the drawn lines. Iron them to brown #2 and cut out each tree, adding a ¼" seam allowance outside each shape.

3. Using the illustration below as a guide, pin the appliqués to the background. Appliqué the trees in place, carefully cut away the background fabric behind each appliqué, and then remove the freezer paper.

FUSING THE MOTIFS

1. Cut motifs from your theme fabrics. Follow the general shape of each motif, leaving an approximate ¼"-wide seam allowance. Pin the motifs in place on the background. Cover the tree branches with leaves, add flowers near the shoreline, and wind vines and small flowers around the tree trunks. Place mountains, houses, or small trees in the distance. You can put fish in the water, and birds or other small animals along the shore. Make the design lush and full.

2. One by one, remove the motifs and iron them to the textured side of fusible web. Follow the manufacturer's instructions to ensure the best possible bond. After the fusible web has cooled, cut out the fused motif along its outline. Score the paper backing with a pin and peel it off. Pin the motif in place on the quilt top.

3. Fuse the motifs in place. Use a press cloth, and don't forget to remove the pins before you press.

EMBROIDERING AND EMBELLISHING

1. Using embroidery floss, perle cotton, or decorative thread, blanket-stitch around each motif (pages 45–47). Use a variety of threads and try changing colors or textures to correspond to the colors of the motifs.

2. Use other embroidery stitches in various threads and colors to embellish the motifs.

3. Using an outline stitch, add winding vines, branches, and tendrils.

4. Stitch silk-ribbon leaves, flowers, buds, and other accents. Embroider additional flowers directly over some of the fused motifs.

5. Use beads to enhance flowers or to add sparkle and shimmer to the water.

6. Sew any buttons you've chosen to the quilt top. You might look for some bird- and fish-shaped buttons, or fruit and insects to add to the trees.

ADDING THE MITERED BORDERS

1. Measure the width and length of your quilt top through the center. It should be approximately 43½" x 45½", but your quilt measurements may vary due to the amount of embroidery and details you've added to your design. Square up the quilt top as needed (page 58).

2. From the light purple fabric for the inner border, cut 5 strips, each 2½" x 42". Sew the strips together end to end, then cut 4 pieces, each 50" long, from the strip.

3. From the white fabric, cut 6 strips, each 1½" x 42". Sew the strips together end to end, then cut 4 pieces, each 60" long, from the strip.

4. From the dark purple fabric, cut 6 strips, each 4½" x 42". Sew the strips together end to end, then cut 4 pieces, each 65" long, from the strip.

5. Fold each border strip in half crosswise and mark the center. Matching center marks, sew a light purple, white, and dark purple strip together to make 1 border unit. The ends of the middle and outer border strips will extend beyond the inner border strip. Don't trim the excess fabric. You'll need it for mitering the corners.

6. Match the center of a border to the center of a quilt-top edge. Pin the border to the quilt and stitch in place, starting and stopping ¼" from the ends of the quilt top. Don't trim the excess fabric.

7. Repeat steps 5 and 6 for each of the borders. After all borders are attached, miter the corners, referring to "Borders" on page 57. Take care to match the seams where the inner, middle, and outer borders meet.

QUILTING AND FINISHING

1. Cut the backing fabric in half to make two 60" pieces. Trim the selvages, then stitch the pieces together. If you plan to quilt by hand, press the seam open to reduce bulk; if you plan to machine quilt, press the seam to one side. Trim the backing to approximately 60" x 62".

2. Layer the backing, batting, and quilt top, then baste them together.

3. Following the design lines on the printed motifs, add quilting to the flowers, petals, leaves, trees, animals, fish, and other motifs.

4. Quilt the background blocks and borders as desired. In my quilt, I used crosshatching and rows of parallel diagonal lines.

5. Cut 6 strips of dark purple fabric for binding. Depending on the thickness of your batting, you may want to cut strips 2" or 2¼" wide. Following the directions in "Binding the Edges" on page 61, sew double-fold binding to your quilt.

6. Referring to "Adding a Hanging Sleeve" on page 61, make a sleeve and attach it to the back of your quilt.

7. Sign and date your work of art.

Bibliography

For more information on basic quilting and rotary-cutting techniques, consult the following sources. These books also contain excellent ideas for pieced backgrounds.

Hopkins, Judy, and Nancy J. Martin. *Rotary Riot: 40 Fast and Fabulous Quilts.* Bothell, Wash.: That Patchwork Place, Inc., 1991.

Martin, Nancy J. *Simply Scrappy Quilts.* Bothell, Wash.: That Patchwork Place, Inc., 1995.

McCloskey, Marsha. *Quick Classic Quilts.* Birmingham, Ala.: Oxmoor House, Inc., 1996.

For more information on broderie perse, embroidery stitches, and silk-ribbon techniques, consult the following sources:

Brown, Elsa. *Creative Quilting.* New York: Watson-Guptill Publications, 1975.

Gostelow, Mary. *A World of Embroidery.* New York: Charles Scribner's Sons, 1975.

Montano, Judith Baker. *Elegant Stitches.* Lafayette, Calif.: C & T Publishing, 1995.

About the Author

JOANNE GOLDSTEIN combines her background in art with a passion for quilting. Her love of fabric, handwork, embellishment, and design has resulted in a creative approach to contemporary quilting. Past ownership of a country craft and quilt shop gave her ample opportunity to experiment with and learn more about her craft.

Joanne's work has been published in quilt magazines and exhibited at several major quilt shows. She is a member of Coral Springs Quilters and The American Quilters Society. Her enthusiasm for developing new ways to combine contemporary techniques with traditional quiltmaking methods is contagious. "Traditional quilts are America's original art form," she says. "Into every contemporary quilt is stitched the voices of our mothers and grandmothers, urging us toward the future, making what was once old new again."

Joanne lives and quilts in Coral Springs, Florida, with her husband, Jerry, and three children: Steven, Lauren, and David.

Books from Martingale & Company

Appliqué
Appliqué in Bloom
Baltimore Bouquets
Basic Quiltmaking Techniques for Hand Appliqué
Basic Quiltmaking Techniques for Machine Appliqué
Coxcomb Quilt
The Easy Art of Appliqué
Folk Art Animals
From a Quilter's Garden
Fun with Sunbonnet Sue
Garden Appliqué
Interlacing Borders
Once Upon a Quilt
Stars in the Garden
Sunbonnet Sue All Through the Year
Welcome to the North Pole

Basic Quiltmaking Techniques
Basic Quiltmaking Techniques for Borders & Bindings
Basic Quiltmaking Techniques for Curved Piecing
Basic Quiltmaking Techniques for Divided Circles
Basic Quiltmaking Techniques for Eight-Pointed Stars
Basic Quiltmaking Techniques for Hand Appliqué
Basic Quiltmaking Techniques for Machine Appliqué
Basic Quiltmaking Techniques for Strip Piecing
Your First Quilt Book (or it should be!)

Crafts
15 Beads
The Art of Handmade Paper and Collage
Christmas Ribbonry
Fabric Mosaics
Folded Fabric Fun
Hand-Stitched Samplers from I Done My Best
The Home Decorator's Stamping Book
Making Memories
A Passion for Ribbonry
Stamp with Style

Design Reference
Color: The Quilter's Guide
Design Essentials: The Quilter's Guide
Design Your Own Quilts
The Nature of Design
QuiltSkills
Surprising Designs from Traditional Quilt Blocks

Foundation/Paper Piecing
Classic Quilts with Precise Foundation Piecing
Crazy but Pieceable
Easy Machine Paper Piecing
Easy Mix & Match Machine Paper Piecing
Easy Paper-Pieced Keepsake Quilts
Easy Paper-Pieced Miniatures
Easy Reversible Vests
Go Wild with Quilts
Go Wild with Quilts—Again!
It's Raining Cats & Dogs
Mariner's Medallion
Paper Piecing the Seasons
A Quilter's Ark
Sewing on the Line
Show Me How to Paper Piece

Home Decorating
Decorate with Quilts & Collections
The Home Decorator's Stamping Book
Living with Little Quilts
Make Room for Quilts
Special-Occasion Table Runners
Stitch & Stencil
Welcome Home: Debbie Mumm
Welcome Home: Kaffe Fassett

Joy of Quilting Series
Borders by Design
The Easy Art of Appliqué
A Fine Finish

Hand-Dyed Fabric Made Easy
Happy Endings
Loving Stitches
Machine Quilting Made Easy
A Perfect Match
Press for Success
Sensational Settings
Shortcuts
The Ultimate Book of Quilt Labels

Knitting
Simply Beautiful Sweaters
Two Sticks and a String
Welcome Home: Kaffe Fassett

Machine Quilting/Sewing
Machine Needlelace
Machine Quilting Made Easy
Machine Quilting with Decorative Threads
Quilting Makes the Quilt
Thread Magic
Threadplay

Miniature/Small Quilts
Celebrate! with Little Quilts
Crazy but Pieceable
Easy Paper-Pieced Miniatures
Fun with Miniature Log Cabin Blocks
Little Quilts All Through the House
Living with Little Quilts
Miniature Baltimore Album Quilts
Small Quilts Made Easy
Small Wonders

Quilting/Finishing Techniques
Borders by Design
The Border Workbook
A Fine Finish
Happy Endings
Interlacing Borders
Loving Stitches
Quilt It!
Quilting Design Sourcebook
Quilting Makes the Quilt
Traditional Quilts with Painless Borders
The Ultimate Book of Quilt Labels

Rotary Cutting/Speed Piecing
101 Fabulous Rotary-Cut Quilts
All-Star Sampler
Around the Block with Judy Hopkins
Bargello Quilts
Basic Quiltmaking Techniques for Strip Piecing
Block by Block
Easy Seasonal Wall Quilts
Easy Star Sampler
Fat Quarter Quilts
The Heirloom Quilt
The Joy of Quilting
More Quilts for Baby
More Strip-Pieced Watercolor Magic
A New Slant on Bargello Quilts
A New Twist on Triangles
Patchwork Pantry
Quilters on the Go
Quilting Up a Storm
Quilts for Baby
Quilts from Aunt Amy
ScrapMania
Simply Scrappy Quilts
Square Dance
Strip-Pieced Watercolor Magic
Stripples Strikes Again!
Strips That Sizzle
Two-Color Quilts

Seasonal Projects
Christmas Ribbonry
Easy Seasonal Wall Quilts

Folded Fabric Fun
Holiday Happenings
Quilted for Christmas
Quilted for Christmas, Book III
Quilted for Christmas, Book IV
A Silk-Ribbon Album
Welcome to the North Pole

Stitchery/Needle Arts
Christmas Ribbonry
Crazy Rags
Hand-Stitched Samplers from I Done My Best
Machine Needlelace
Miniature Baltimore Album Quilts
A Passion for Ribbonry
A Silk-Ribbon Album
Victorian Elegance

Surface Design/Fabric Manipulation
15 Beads
The Art of Handmade Paper and Collage
Complex Cloth
Creative Marbling on Fabric
Dyes & Paints
Hand-Dyed Fabric Made Easy
Jazz It Up

Theme Quilts
The Cat's Meow
Everyday Angels in Extraordinary Quilts
Fabric Collage Quilts
Fabric Mosaics
Folded Fabric Fun
Folk Art Quilts
Honoring the Seasons
It's Raining Cats & Dogs
Life in the Country with Country Threads
Making Memories
More Quilts for Baby
The Nursery Rhyme Quilt
Once Upon a Quilt
Patchwork Pantry
Quilted Landscapes
Quilting Your Memories
Quilts for Baby
Quilts from Nature
Through the Window and Beyond
Two-Color Quilts

Watercolor Quilts
More Strip-Pieced Watercolor Magic
Strip-Pieced Watercolor Magic
Watercolor Impressions
Watercolor Quilts

Wearables
Crazy Rags
Dress Daze
Easy Reversible Vests
Jacket Jazz Encore
Just Like Mommy
Variations in Chenille

Many of these books are available through your local quilt, fabric, craft-supply, or art-supply store. For more information, call, write, fax, or e-mail for our free full-color catalog.

Martingale & Company
PO Box 118
Bothell, WA 98041-0118 USA

1-800-426-3126
International: 1-425-483-3313
24-Hour Fax: 1-425-486-7596
Web site: www.patchwork.com
E-mail: info@martingale-pub.com

3/99